GIN MADE
ME DO IT

GIN MADE ME DO IT

60 BEAUTIFULLY BOTANICAL COCKTAILS

JASSY DAVIS
ILLUSTRATED BY RUBY TAYLOR

HarperCollins*Publishers*

HarperCollins*Publishers*
1 London Bridge Street
London SE1 9GF
www.harpercollins.co.uk

First published by HarperCollins*Publishers* in 2018

10

Copyright © HarperCollins*Publishers*
Written by Jassy Davis
Illustrated by Ruby Taylor
Designed by Gareth Butterworth

A catalogue record for this book is available from the British Library

ISBN 978-0-00-828030-7

Printed and bound in Latvia

MIX
Paper from
responsible sources

FSC
www.fsc.org

FSC™ C007454

CONTENTS

A SHORT AND SCANDALOUS HISTORY OF GIN

It began with monks – 11th-century Benedictine monks, to be specific. They lived in Salerno, in southern Italy, in a monastery surrounded by rolling hills and juniper trees. And they had a still. A swan-necked alembic still; the kind invented by Abu Musa Jabir ibn Hayyan in Baghdad in the late 700s, and the kind you might find in your local gin distillery today. The monks used it to distil sharp, fiery, alcoholic tonics, one of which was distilled from wine infused with juniper berries. It wasn't exactly gin – not as we know it – but it was the first recorded juniper-scented spirit.

The monks didn't consider themselves early mixologists. They were making medicines, hence the juniper. As a medicinal herb, juniper had been an essential part of doctors' kits for centuries: the Romans burned juniper branches for purification and medieval plague doctors stuffed the beaks of their ghoulish masks with juniper to protect them from the Black Death. Across Europe, apothecaries handed out juniper tonic wines for coughs, colds, pains, strains, ruptures and cramps. These were a popular cure-all. A little too popular, according to some, who thought people were keener to take their medicine than they should be.

THE RISE OF THE DISTILLERY

By the mid-16th century, alchemists had worked out how to distil spirits cheaply from grain. In Holland, good harvests filled the barns and burgeoning trade routes brought spices from South East Asia in incredible quantities. By adding those spices and plenty of locally grown juniper to cheap malt spirit, the Dutch created an inexpensive brew that grew and grew in popularity. They called it genever.

The Dutch took genever around the world, but it was Elizabeth I who accidentally brought it to England. She sent soldiers to help the Dutch fight for independence in 1585 and they returned with bottles of the aromatic drink. The English quickly developed a taste for it, and by 1621, London had over 200 distilleries busy making 'strong and hot waters' for a thirsty public. When the Dutch Prince William of Orange landed in Devon in 1688 and marched to London to take the throne, genever's place in English society was guaranteed.

In 1710, 2 million gallons of spirits were drunk in England and Wales. By 1743 it was over 8 million. Most of it was drunk in cities, and nowhere loved gin more than London, where 90% of all English spirits were distilled. Daniel Defoe, who had written a pamphlet in 1726 for the London Company of Distillers praising malt spirits, complained in 1728 that people were getting 'so drunk on a Sunday they cannot work for a day or two following'. A gin-fuelled crime wave spilled into the streets and courts. The newspapers were scandalised and the government forced into action.

A series of Gin Acts passed between 1729 and 1738 raised duty on gin and the cost of a distilling licence. Legal gin sales dropped, while juniper tonics made by surgeons became mysteriously more popular and the bootleggers were busier than ever. Informers ran protection rackets, mobs lynched suspected informers, and gin shops sold cheap hooch flavoured with turpentine and sulphuric acid to the gin-crazed masses.

Finally, in 1743 a Gin Act was passed that made a difference. Under it, licences were easier to buy and duty easier to collect. The government gave up on prohibition and the black market gave up on gin. Legal and perhaps even respectable, gin lost its cachet with the drinking classes.

It didn't vanish entirely though, and in the early 19th century, a round of tax cuts slashed duty on spirits and whetted the public's appetite for gin once more. Within a year the amount of gin drunk in the country had doubled, and gin drinkers had somewhere new to go to indulge in their favourite spirit: the gin palace. The opposite of a seedy gin shop, gin palaces were handsome buildings, clad in wood and glass, and shining with light. They were oases of warmth and conviviality amid the chill Victorian nights.

COCKTAIL CULTURE

The quality of the gin itself was changing too. The 18th-century 'Old Tom' gins had been made in alembic pot stills, which had to be cleaned between batches, and produced rough spirits that had to be disguised with sugar and lots of botanicals. The Coffey still, invented in 1831, could be run continuously and produced a lighter, fresher, more consistent spirit. This smoother, clean-tasting gin came to be known as London dry. Old Tom gin sales declined, and in America, where the first cocktails were being shaken up, London dry was the spirit of choice for martinis, slings and fizzes.

However, America was about to prove that no one ever learns anything from history. The Temperance Movement had been campaigning for a ban on alcohol since the 1820s. In 1919 they got their wish: the Volstead Act prohibited the drinking of any beverage stronger than 0.5% alcohol by volume. As in 18th-century England, so in 20th-century America. Instead of giving up booze, drinkers went underground. In speakeasies, which ranged from dingy rooms with a couple of chairs to spectacular clubs like the Dil Pickle and the Krazy Kat, drinkers kicked back with a heady mix of cocktails and jazz. Gin, easy to make and even easier to mix in strongly flavoured drinks, was riding high. Bootleggers turned industrial spirit into 'bathtub gin', while smugglers snuck cases of gin across the US borders. By the 1930s, alcohol-consumption rates were actually higher than they had been in 1919, and it was obvious that Prohibition had failed. In 1933, the 21st Amendment repealed Prohibition, and in the White House, Franklin D. Roosevelt celebrated by mixing martinis.

Post-Prohibition, cocktails moved out of the bar and into the home. Drinks parties were a chic way to mix and mingle, until World War II, that is. Drinkers in the US could still buy good-quality gin and whiskey, but in Britain shortages meant it was back to rough spirits and the taste of turpentine. After the war, gin struggled. A new generation turned to vodka to fuel their fun. Neutral-tasting, easy to drink and supposedly undetectable on your breath, it seemed more modern than gin, with its seedy past and aromatic flavour. Women swapped G&Ts to become VATGirls (vodka and tonics), and by the 1980s, gin was something you only kept around for your aunties at Christmas time.

All seemed lost for gin, until Bombay Sapphire was launched in 1988. Made to a 1761 recipe, boasting ten botanicals and sold in a stylish blue glass bottle, this was worlds away from the fusty bottles of gin the public had got used to. The gin market was suddenly a space

where distillers could experiment. In the US, nearly 100 craft gin distilleries opened between 1990 and 2000. In the UK, laws that had stopped small-batch distilleries opening were slowly repealed. Since then, distilleries have opened across the country offering not just elegantly made London dry gins, but craft gins flavoured with hundreds of different botanicals, and even Old Tom gins have had a resurgence.

Gin has been around for more than 1,000 years, but there's never been a better time to be a gin drinker than right now.

MEET MADAME GENEVA

In 1736, London gin drinkers dressed in black held a mock funeral for 'Madame Geneva', the spirit they loved and that they were afraid would be killed by the 1736 Gin Act. They were wrong, of course. Like Obi-Wan Kenobi, attempts to strike gin down only make it more powerful. Today the range of gins in your local bottle shop is so vast, it's worth learning about the common styles so you can be sure to pick the perfect bottle for every occasion.

LONDON DRY GIN

The first thing you should know about London dry gin is that it doesn't have to be made in London. London dry is a method, not a place, and it's protected under EU law. To be a London dry gin, a grain spirit must be distilled in a traditional still with natural ingredients, and no flavourings, colour or sugar can be added once it has been distilled. It has a minimum ABV of 37.5% and juniper is the predominate flavour. Fresh, citrusy and, obviously, dry, London dry is a classic style of gin that's perfect for mixing in G&Ts and cocktails.

NEW WESTERN DRY GIN

Also called craft gin, artisan gin, boutique gin and small-batch gin. By EU law, new western dry gins should probably be called 'distilled gin'. They're gins that are made in a traditional still with natural flavourings, but once they're distilled, flavourings, additives and colourings can be added. The emphasis in new western dry gins is less on juniper and more on the other botanicals, which are often added after the gin has been distilled. Hendricks, Tanqueray No. Ten, Aviation and G Vine are all examples of new western dry. Each has its own unique flavour profile, so when you find the gin you love, keep hold of it and experiment to find the cocktails that its mix of botanicals best suits.

PLYMOUTH GIN

While London dry gins don't have to be made in London, Plymouth gin can only be distilled in Plymouth, Devon. There's just one distillery doing that called, naturally enough, Plymouth Gin. The distillery was established in 1793 and for 200 years it supplied gin to the British Royal Navy. After the distillery was bombed in 1941, the Navy ended the contract and the distillery had a few lean years until it was rescued by investors in 1996. The flavour is sweeter and earthier than London dry. At first sip, it's heavy on the coriander and has a lingering spicy note of liquorice. When you're making 19th-century navy cocktails, like Pink Gin (see page 60), reach for Plymouth first.

NAVY STRENGTH GIN

In the 18th century, there was one sure way to make certain the barrels of gin being loaded onto ships contained the real thing, and hadn't been watered down or adulterated: spill the gin on some gunpowder. If the gunpowder still lit, the gin was 114 proof, or 57% ABV as we know it now. There's no specific flavour profile for navy strength gins. The only thing that unites them is their alcoholic strength, so try a few to find the gin that suits you. The first time you make a Gimlet (see page 55), that quintessential British navy mix of gin and lime juice, make it with Plymouth navy strength.

OLD TOM GIN

The gin that bridges the gap between Dutch genevers and London dry, Old Tom gins emerged in the 18th century when London's distillers were making gin in unreliable pot stills that produced a rough spirit. By being heavy-handed with sugar and liquorice, the distillers made their gin passable enough for London's drinking classes. The gin renaissance has seen a few distilleries start producing Old Tom gins again and they have a malty, sweet flavour with a more muted juniper profile than London dry. Use it to make Tom Collins and Martinez cocktails (see pages 28 and 40, respectively).

OUDE GENEVER

The granddaddy of gin, genever can only be made in Belgium, The Netherlands and parts of France and Germany. Oude, as you may have guessed, means 'old'. But it isn't a barrel-aged spirit. The 'old' refers to the method, and oude genever is an old-style, traditional genever. That it's juniper-scented goes without saying, but oude genevers are also 15–50% malt wine (the rest has to be a neutral grain spirit), so they have a malty flavour with a rich, viscous mouthfeel. Try it neat as a digestif, or mixed in cocktails in place of Old Tom gin, whiskey or bourbon.

JONGE GENEVER

Oude genever's young, thrusting, more modern sibling, jonge genever was invented in the 1950s as a response to the rising popularity of vodka. Jonge genever is 15% malt wine mixed with a neutral grain spirit and it tastes more like a classic dry gin. Mix it in Negronis, Last Words and Puritans in place of London dry.

To make gin, a base spirit is distilled (usually from grains), then it is redistilled with botanicals to extract the essential oils and add flavour. Redistilling is most commonly done by the 'steep and boil' method, wherein a watered down base spirit is steeped with juniper and other botanicals for up to 48 hours, then distilled through a pot still and mixed with water until it hits the right ABV. The redistilling can also be done by vapourising the base spirit through the aromatics.

In a traditional pot still, the stillman has a lot of influence over the process as he or she has to make the 'cuts'. Because different botanicals evaporate at different temperatures, the stillman has to find the moment in the process when the right mix of flavours all come together. The first runnings out of the still, called the heads, have to be cut just as the sweet-scented heart of the run begins to flow, eventually dwindling down to the tails, which also have to be cut. Knowing when to cut the gin is as much art as it is science.

INFUSE YOUR BOOZE

Some of the cocktails in this book call for flavoured gin. There are lots of commercially made flavoured gins (and all of the flavours in this book are available in shops), but it's easy to make your own infused gins at home if you prefer. I use a London dry gin as the base spirit when I'm making infusions. And while I don't use the best small-batch, artisanal craft gin to make them, I also avoid the cheap, bargain basement bottles of spirits that only just qualify as gin. If you'd drink it in a G&T on a Wednesday night, then it will be good enough for these infusions.

Rhubarb Gin (makes approximately 900ml/30fl oz)
400g (14oz) rhubarb
250g (8oz) caster sugar
2 tbsp freshly squeezed lemon juice
700ml (24fl oz) London dry gin

Wash and trim the rhubarb and chop it into 2 centimetre (¾in) chunks. Scoop into a sterilised 1½ litre (50fl oz) jar. Add the sugar and lemon juice. Seal the jar and give it a good shake, then leave it to steep for 24 hours – this will draw the juices out of the rhubarb. After 24 hours, pour in the gin, seal the jar again and leave to steep somewhere dark and dry for 2 weeks. After 2 weeks, strain the gin through a sieve. Discard the rhubarb and pour the gin back into the jar or a sterilised bottle.

Raspberry Gin (makes approximately 800ml/27fl oz)
250g (8oz) raspberries
100g (3½oz) caster sugar
700ml (24fl oz) London dry gin

Drop the raspberries and sugar into a 1 litre (34fl oz) sterilised jar. Pour in the gin. Seal the jar and leave it to steep somewhere dark and dry for 2 weeks. Give the jar a shake every few days to help dissolve the sugar. After no more than 2 weeks, strain the gin. Discard the raspberries and pour the gin back into the jar or into a sterilised bottle.

Clementine Gin (makes approximately 900ml/30fl oz)
3 large (or 5 small) clementines
200g (7oz) caster sugar
700ml (24fl oz) London dry gin

Quarter the clementines, keeping the skin on, and add them to a sterilised 1½ litre (50fl oz) jar. Add the sugar and gin, seal the jar and leave it to steep somewhere dark and dry for 2 weeks. Give the jar a shake every few days to help dissolve the sugar. After 2 weeks, strain through a sieve. Discard the clementines and pour the gin back into the jar or into a sterilised bottle. If you leave this gin for 3 weeks, the flavour of the pith will come through and it will have a more marmalady flavour. Don't steep it for longer than 3 weeks or it will become bitter.

Earl Grey Gin (makes approximately 700ml/24fl oz)
4 tbsp Earl Grey loose leaf tea
700ml (24fl oz) London dry gin

Drop the Earl Grey into an 800 millilitre (27fl oz) sterilised jar and pour in the gin. Seal the jar and leave it to steep for no more than 2 hours. After 2 hours, strain the gin through a sieve. Discard the tea and pour the gin back into the jar or into a sterilised bottle.

Sloe Gin (makes approximately 850ml/28fl oz)
400g (14oz) sloes
2 almonds
125g (4½oz) caster sugar
700ml (24fl oz) London dry gin

Prepare your sloes by pricking them all over with a sterilised needle or putting them in a freezerproof tub or bag and freezing them for 48 hours to crack them. Tip the sloes into a 1½ litre (50fl oz)

14

sterilised jar. Lightly crush the almonds and add them to the jar with the sugar. Pour in the gin. Seal the jar and leave it to steep somewhere dark and dry for 3–12 months. Shake the jar every few days during the first couple of weeks to help dissolve the sugar. After at least 3 months, strain the gin through a sieve and taste it. If it's too tart for your taste, stir in a little Simple Syrup (see below) until it's sweet enough. Pour back into the jar or a sterilised bottle.

Simple Syrup (makes approximately 200ml/7fl oz)

When you're first tasting an infused gin, it's a good idea to have some sugar syrup like this on hand, in case the gin isn't quite sweet enough. It's also handy for making cocktails, as it's much easier to mix than plain sugar.

100g (3½oz) caster sugar
100ml (3½fl oz) water

Combine the sugar and water in a small saucepan. Gently heat, stirring until the sugar dissolves. Bring to the boil, then turn down the heat and simmer for 2 minutes. Take off the heat and leave to cool. Pour the syrup into a sterilised jar, seal and store in the fridge for up to 2 weeks.

You can also add flavour to your Simple Syrup with herbs (see page 139), or aromatics (see page 135) for an extra dimension.

THE PERFECT MARTINI

Before we start experimenting with other cocktails, we need to talk about martinis. Shorthand for elegance, sophistication, debauchery, vice and pleasure, martinis are the cocktails most novice drinkers aspire to. The perfect mix of fire and ice, martinis are urban cool, liquid satin silver bullets served in frosted glasses.

There are plenty of tall tales associated with the origins of the martini. The most famous concerns legendary barman 'Professor' Jerry Thomas, who mixed drinks around the US and wrote the 1862 *Bar-Tender's Guide*, the first ever cocktail book. The story goes that Thomas was keeping bar in San Francisco when a tired, dusty traveller came in and asked for something new to drink. Thomas asked where he was heading and the traveller said Martinez. So Thomas mixed together gin, vermouth and bitters and called it the Martinez, which was later shortened to martini.

It's a neat story, but it doesn't seem to be any more true than the claim that the drink was made in honour of the Martini-Henry rifle or named after the Italian vermouth brand, Martini. The first actual martini recipe appeared in print in 1888, in Harry Johnson's *Bartender's Manual*, although that recipe still used sweet Italian vermouth rather than the dry French vermouth preferred today.

Martinis were the mainstay of cocktail parties in the early part of the 20th century and adventurous drinkers liked to put their own twists on the drink. The occultist Aleister Crowley, added laudanum to his martinis. Others played with the ratios of gin to vermouth, moving away from the wet mixture of four parts gin to one part vermouth to drier ratios of 7:1, 10:1 or, in the case of Winston Churchill, no vermouth at all.

As martinis evolved, a debate raged on: shaken or stirred? The main argument against shaking is that it 'bruises' the gin, which doesn't seem likely as gin doesn't have any capillaries to burst. What shaking does do is make the drink cloudy as little chips of ice break up and get muddled in with the liquid. For an ice-cold martini as clear as a lake in winter, stirring is the only way to go.

HOW TO MAKE A MARTINI

Below are two recipes for a martini, one dry with a ratio of 6:1, and a wetter version with a ratio closer to 3:1. For the vermouth, use a dry French vermouth like Dolin or Noilly Prat. For the gin, use your favourite – just make sure it's good quality. A martini is no place to hide a bottle of cheap booze.

Dry Martini

10ml (⅓fl oz) dry French vermouth
60ml (2fl oz) good-quality gin
1 dash of orange bitters (optional)

Place your martini glass into the freezer for at least 30 minutes, or fill it with ice to chill. Half fill a mixing glass with ice and pour in the vermouth. Stir a few times to coat the ice. Pour in the gin and add a dash of orange bitters (the bitters are optional, but I like them in a dry martini to add a little extra flavour). Stir for 30 seconds, then strain the martini into your chilled glass, garnish as desired (see page 18) and serve.

Wet Martini

15ml (½fl oz) dry French vermouth
50ml (1¾fl oz) good-quality gin

Place your martini glass into the freezer for at least 30 minutes, or fill it with ice to chill. Half fill a mixing glass with ice and pour in the vermouth. Stir a few times to coat the ice then pour in the gin. Stir for 30 seconds, then strain the martini into your chilled glass, garnish and serve.

LEARN THE LINGO

With a twist

Garnished with a twist of lemon zest. This is the classic martini garnish and the peel is usually twisted over the top of the martini to spritz the surface with citrus oils before being dropped into the glass.

With an olive

The more savoury alternative to a twist. Plain green olives either dropped in or skewered on a cocktail stick and laid in the glass. Stuffed olives are for eating on the side of your martini, not putting in it.

Dirty Martini

A martini with a dash of olive brine added to the mix, usually around 1 teaspoon.

Gibson

A martini garnished with cocktail onions. To make at home, skewer 2–3 silverskin pickled onions on a cocktail stick and lay in the glass (or just drop them straight in).

Navy

A martini made with navy strength gin. Because it's so boozy, this is a martini best served super chilled. Make sure all the ingredients are ice cold, then give them a good stir with ice, strain and serve.

Burnt

A martini with a splash of whisky. Follow the recipe for a wet martini, but use a mix of 8 millilitres (¼fl oz) dry French vermouth and 8 millilitres (¼fl oz) peaty Scottish whisky. Garnish with olives or an orange twist.

In and out

A martini with just a hint of vermouth. You can make it by filling your martini glass with ice, adding a splash of vermouth and swirling it around the glass to coat. Mix your gin with ice to chill, dump the ice and vermouth out of the glass and strain the gin in. Alternatively, you can add the vermouth to the ice in the mixing glass as per the recipes on page 17, swirl to coat the ice then strain the vermouth out before adding the gin.

Montgomery

Supposedly Ernest Hemingway's favourite way of preparing a martini. The Montgomery is named after the British Field Marshal, Bernard 'Monty' Montgomery, who liked the gin in his martini to outnumber the vermouth in the same way he liked to outnumber his enemies on the battlefield: 15:1.

THE RECIPES

21

WHITE LADY

One of the greatest literary collaborations of the 20th
century was not a book, but a cocktail. In the 1920s,
Ernest Hemingway and F. Scott Fitzgerald both lived in
Paris and, like all writers, they spent a lot of their time at
the bar. At Harry's New York Bar (called that, even though
it was in Paris), they found Harry MacElhone mixing drinks.
Back in London, MacElhone had mixed crème de menthe,
Cointreau and lemon juice together to make something
like a White Lady. In Paris, with two infamous literary
boozehounds making suggestions, he swapped the crème
de menthe for gin. A few years later, back in London, The
Savoy's bartender Harry Craddock added egg white
to bring the drink together. It was named after Zelda
Fitzgerald, a Jazz-Age It Girl and a platinum blonde.

Ingredients
45ml (1 ½fl oz) London dry gin
22ml (¾fl oz) Cointreau
22ml (¾fl oz) freshly squeezed lemon juice
15ml (½fl oz) Simple Syrup (see page 15)
15ml (½fl oz) egg white
a lemon twist, to garnish

Instructions
Pour the gin, Cointreau, lemon juice and Simple Syrup
into an ice-filled cocktail shaker. Shake for 30 seconds
to chill, then strain the liquid into a glass, discard the ice
and add the cocktail mix back to the shaker. Pour in the
egg white. Shake again for 30 seconds (this is called a
reverse dry shake and ensures a fluffy finish). Strain into
a chilled coupe glass and garnish with a lemon twist.

BREAKFAST MARTINI

The Breakfast Martini is the signature drink of London
bar scene supremo, Salvatore Calabrese. He invented
the Breakfast Martini in the 1990s, inspired by breakfast
with his wife Sue. Being Italian, Calabrese's preferred
breakfast is a shot of inky black espresso, but one morning
his wife persuaded him to sit down and eat breakfast
with her – tea, toast and marmalade. Inspired, he went
into work at the Library Bar in The Lanesborough Hotel
and mixed the first Breakfast Martini. I've swapped
in clementine gin to up the marmalade notes, but a
London dry or citrusy craft gin will work just as well.

Ingredients
50ml (1¾fl oz) Clementine Gin (see page 14)
15ml (½fl oz) triple sec
15ml (½fl oz) freshly squeezed lemon juice
1 heaped tsp orange marmalade
an orange twist, to garnish

Instructions
Pour all the ingredients into a shaker and stir well to dissolve
the marmalade. Add ice and give it a really good shake. Strain
into a chilled martini glass and garnish with an orange twist.

THE LAST WORD

Proof that a good cocktail will never be forgotten, The Last Word was invented in the 1920s in the Detroit Athletic Club. Prohibition being in force, the drink was made with bathtub gin, and the mix of green chartreuse, maraschino liqueur and lime juice was sharp and sweet enough to smooth out the gin's rougher edges. Post-Prohibition, the cocktail fell out of favour until a bartender at the Zig Zag Café in Seattle, Murray Stenson, picked up a copy of Ted Saucier's 1950s cocktail book *Bottoms Up* and rediscovered the recipe. Stenson put it on the menu in 2004 and within a few years The Last Word was back on bar menus around the world.

Ingredients
22ml (¾fl oz) gin
22ml (¾fl oz) green chartreuse
22ml (¾fl oz) maraschino liqueur
22ml (¾fl oz) freshly squeezed lime juice
a maraschino cherry and a lime twist, to garnish

Instructions
Pour the gin, chartreuse, maraschino liqueur and lime juice into an ice-filled cocktail shaker. Shake well, then strain into a small coupe glass. Drop in a maraschino cherry and garnish with a lime twist.

TOM COLLINS

'Have you seen Tom Collins?'
So went the opening line to a prank that took New
York by storm in 1874. A man would tell his friend that
a certain Tom Collins had been going about town
spreading nasty lies about him, and that if he wanted
to settle the matter, he would find Tom Collins in this
or that bar. His friend would stomp off, outraged. But
when he got to the distant bar, no Tom Collins could
be found. That was, until an entrepreneurial bartender
invented a drink called the Tom Collins. When furious
men walked into his bar and demanded Tom Collins,
he poured them the drink and charged them for it.
That's one story anyway. John Collins, a barman working
in London in the late 1880s, also claimed credit for the
iconic recipe, as did a Mr Collins of the Whitehouse Tavern
in 1870s New York, and as have many more Collinses
the world over. That's the trouble with Tom Collins –
you can never pin him down and find out the truth.

Ingredients
60ml (2fl oz) Old Tom gin
30ml (1fl oz) freshly squeezed lemon juice
15ml (½fl oz) Simple Syrup (see page 15)
120ml (4fl oz) soda water
an orange slice and a maraschino cherry, to garnish

Instructions
Pour the gin, lemon juice and Simple Syrup into an
ice-filled cocktail shaker. Give it a vigorous shake.
Fill a large highball glass with ice and strain the gin
mix into it. Top up with soda water and garnish with
an orange slice and a maraschino cherry.

CORPSE REVIVER NUMBER 2

Corpse revivers are a class of drink dating back to the late 1800s, when cocktails were just becoming popular and were drunk more often in the morning than the evening. These cocktails harked back to medieval tonics, but instead of warding off diseases, they combatted hangovers. Harry Craddock included two recipes for Corpse Revivers in *The Savoy Cocktail Book*, first published in 1930. The Number 1 was based around Cognac, while Number 2 used gin. Zesty and astringent, it's strong enough to perk up the most muddle-headed drinker, although, as Craddock warns, 'Four of these taken in quick succession will unrevive the corpse again'.

Ingredients
1 dash of absinthe
22ml (¾fl oz) London dry gin
22ml (¾fl oz) Lillet Blanc (or Aperitivo
    Cocchi Americano, which is a bit closer
    in flavour to Kina Lillet, the original ingredient)
22ml (¾fl oz) triple sec
22ml (¾fl oz) freshly squeezed lemon juice
an orange twist, to garnish

Instructions
Add a dash of absinthe to a chilled martini glass. Turn the glass to rinse the sides with the absinthe, then tip any excess into a cocktail shaker. Add the gin, Lillet Blanc, triple sec, lemon juice and ice to the shaker and shake vigorously together. Strain into the glass, garnish with an orange twist and serve.

GIN & IT

One of the many drinks that can claim to be a precursor to the martini, the 'it' in Gin & It is Italian – Italian red vermouth. In New York in the 1880s it was called a sweet martini, and the drink made its way to Britain in 1887 when the bar at the American Exhibition in London served gin and sweet vermouth to drinkers looking for something new and stylish to sip.

Ingredients
45ml (1 ½fl oz) gin
45ml (1 ½fl oz) sweet vermouth
1 dash of Angostura bitters
an orange twist, to garnish

Instructions
Half fill a mixing glass with ice. Pour in the gin and sweet vermouth and add a dash of bitters. Stir for about 15 seconds, then strain into a martini glass. Garnish with an orange twist.

BRAMBLE

The Bramble was invented by Dick Bradsell in the 1980s when he was working at Fred's Club in Soho, London. As he tells it himself, he woke up one day wanting to create a truly 'British' gin cocktail. Some experimenting led him to the Bramble, named for the blackberry bushes he scraped his knees on as a child on the Isle of Wight. It's not entirely British due to the crème de mure and lemon juice (although you can get good British blackberry liqueurs these days, Britain is still yet to grow its own lemons), but it does have something of the crisp sweetness of those British end-of-summer days, when blackberries hang heavy in the hedgerows.

Ingredients
60ml (2fl oz) Plymouth gin
30ml (1fl oz) freshly squeezed lemon juice
15ml (½fl oz) Simple Syrup (see page 15)
15ml (½fl oz) crème de mure
a couple of blackberries, to garnish

Instructions
Fill an old fashioned glass with crushed ice. Pour the gin, lemon juice and Simple Syrup over the ice and gently stir together. Top up with crushed ice so it fills the glass again. Pour the crème de mure over the top so it 'bleeds' down into the drink. Top with a couple of blackberries and serve with two short straws. (The straws are traditional, but plastic straws are so bad for the environment, I prefer to skip tradition and give this cocktail a stir before serving.)

THE PURITAN

A turn-of-the-century cocktail invented around 1900, it takes its lead from the martini and – whisper it – I actually prefer a Puritan. The chartreuse and orange bitters add a dash of sweetness that enhances the mix of aromatics in the vermouth and gin, making the Puritan an altogether more interesting drink. It's a classic that seems to have fallen out of fashion, but I'm hopeful a bartender will rediscover it, put it on the menu and get people drinking it again.

Ingredients
45ml (1½fl oz) London dry gin
15ml (½fl oz) dry vermouth
8ml (¼fl oz) yellow chartreuse
1 dash of orange bitters
an orange twist, to garnish

Instructions
Half fill a mixing glass with ice. Pour in all the ingredients and stir together for 30 seconds. Strain into a chilled martini glass and serve with an orange twist.

CHARTREUSE

CHARTREUSE

LIQUEUR FABRIQUÉE
PAR LES PERES   CHARTREUX

1605   L. Garnier

Product of France
ALC 40% BY VOL   750 ML

CHARTREUSE DIFFUSION

ESPRESSO MARTINI

In 1983, Dick Bradsell was mixing drinks at the Soho Brasserie in London, when a famous model (Bradsell never disclosed who) walked up to the bar and asked for a drink that would 'wake me up, then **** me up'. Bradsell shook a fresh espresso with vodka, Tia Maria, Kahlúa and sugar syrup and strained it into a martini glass, calling it a Vodka Espresso. Subsequently, he tweaked the recipe to perfect his Espresso Martini and I've given it a go-over of my own, swapping vodka for gin. The sweetness of Old Tom or the clean sharpness of a jonge genever are good stand-ins for vodka, and you can use either Tia Maria or Kahlúa or a mix of both – I like Tia Maria for its darker, more bitter coffee flavour. One essential is fresh espresso – the crema on top of a freshly pulled shot of espresso helps create that fluffy, creamy foam layer on top of the finished cocktail. The usual garnish is three coffee beans, but I like a shake of cocoa powder too for a faux cappuccino finish.

Ingredients
50ml (1¾fl oz) Old Tom gin or jonge genever
22ml (¾fl oz) Tia Maria or Kahlúa
22ml (¾fl oz) hot, fresh espresso
3 coffee beans and cocoa powder (optional), to garnish

Instructions
Half fill a cocktail shaker with ice and pour in the gin, Tia Maria or Kahlúa and espresso. Shake together vigorously for 30 seconds, then strain into a chilled martini glass. Top with 3 coffee beans and a little dusting of cocoa powder, if using.

MARTINEZ

The drink that begat the martini. Possibly. But probably
not. We've already met 'Professor' Jerry Thomas and his
shaky claim to have invented the Martinez on page 16.
The problem with Thomas's claim is that his recipe for the
Martinez appeared in the 1887 edition of his *Bar-Tender's
Guide*, which was published two years after his death. And
Thomas, who modestly described himself as 'the Jupiter
Olympus of the bar', was not one to keep quiet about
his inventions, so it seems unlikely he'd have kept schtum
about inventing this drink. The first known Martinez recipe
was published in O. H. Byron's 1884 book, *The Modern
Bartender*, although it's not much of a recipe. Just one line
at the bottom of a page, saying: 'Same as Manhattan,
only you substitute gin for whiskey.' That description gives
you an idea of the cocktail's flavour. It's a murky mix
of bitter herbs, orange zest and cherry stones that's a
world away from the glacial sharpness of a dry martini
and has a glamorous, grown-up appeal all of its own.

Ingredients
60ml (2fl oz) Old Tom gin
30ml (1fl oz) sweet vermouth
8ml (¼fl oz) curaçao
8ml (¼fl oz) maraschino liqueur
1 dash of Angostura bitters
a lemon twist, to garnish

Instructions
Half fill a mixing glass with ice. Add all the ingredients
and stir for around 30 seconds. Strain into a chilled
coupe glass and garnish with a lemon twist.

MARASCHINO

LIQUEUR

ITALY

200ml

MARASCHINO

LIQUEUR

ITALY

aromatic bitters

ANGOSTURA

200ml

MARASCHINO

LIQUEUR

ITALY

VESPER MARTINI

James Bond's original drink of choice is not a cocktail for the novice drinker. In *Casino Royale,* Bond gives the recipe: 'Three measures of Gordon's, one of vodka, half a measure of Kina Lillet; shake it very well until it's ice cold, then add a large thin slice of lemon peel'. CIA bagman Felix Leiter is goggle-eyed at Bond's booze-heavy concoction, but James reassures Felix he can handle it, telling him: 'This drink's my own invention. I'm going to patent it when I can think of a good name.' And think of it he does when he meets the beautiful, doomed double agent Vesper Lynd. Since the 1950s Gordon's has reduced its ABV to 37%, and Kina Lillet is no longer available, so to mix up something Bond wouldn't raise an eyebrow at, use a London dry gin with an ABV of at least 40% and swap in Aperitivo Cocchi Americano for the Kina Lillet. It's flavoured with cinchona, the bitter bark that gave Kina Lillet its tart quinine taste and is the closest thing on the market to the original aperitif. If you can't find it, go for Lillet Blanc.

Ingredients
60ml (2fl oz) London dry gin
22ml (¾fl oz) vodka
8ml (¼fl oz) Aperitivo Cocchi Americano or Lillet Blanc
a lemon twist, to garnish

Instructions
Pour all the ingredients into an ice-filled cocktail shaker. Shake together until the liquid is ice cold, then double strain into a chilled martini glass – double straining means straining your martini out of the shaker and through a fine mesh sieve into the glass. This helps catch any tiny chips of ice that could cloud your martini. Garnish with a lemon twist to serve.

AVIATION

The first Aviation recipe appeared in Hugo R. Ensslin's 1917
Recipes for Mixed Drinks, just as the golden age of aviation
was dawning. In essence, it's a gin sour but with sweet
maraschino liqueur rather than sugar syrup balancing out
the lemon's astringent bite. The crème de violette turns the
drink a pale blue colour, tinged with lilac. With a dark red
maraschino cherry sinking to the bottom of the glass like the
setting sun, there's more than a hint of endless summer skies
about this drink. It's why I would never double strain it – the
cloudy swirl of ice and the froth of the bubbles resting on
top are too full of life to be fastidiously sieved away from this
drink, which is all about soaring away, up, up and into the air.

Ingredients
50ml (1¾fl oz) Old Tom gin
15ml (½fl oz) freshly squeezed lemon juice
15ml (½fl oz) maraschino liqueur
8ml (¼fl oz) crème de violette
a maraschino cherry, to garnish

Instructions
Half fill a cocktail shaker with ice and pour in all the
liquid ingredients. Shake together well and strain into a
martini glass. Drop in a maraschino cherry and serve.

GIN & TONIC

In the 1990s, bucking the vodka-cranberry trend, I drank gin and tonic. Everybody laughed at this because G&Ts were grandma drinks – dusty, fusty, old fashioned things. In pubs there was only ever one choice of gin, and it was meanly squirted into a stubby glass with a miserly rattle of ice cubes and a thin, wizened slice of lemon. How things have changed. Bars today line up rows of gem-coloured bottles of gin and boast about their range. Bartenders tailor the garnish to the gin, and you're as likely to get your G&T in a goldfish-bowl-sized Spanish copa glass as a highball with sturdy sides and branded etchings. My years of patiently sipping G&Ts have finally been rewarded – hallelujah! When it comes to making a G&T at home, use a roomy glass and pack it with ice. The more ice, the slower it melts and the less it dilutes your drink. I like a 1:2 ratio of gin to tonic, so I can feel the gin's edge without falling over it too quickly. And as for garnishes: the world is your lemon. Pick something that chimes with the botanicals in your gin to bring out the flavour.

Ingredients
60ml (2fl oz) gin
120ml (4fl oz) tonic water
to garnish: pick from lemon wedges, lime wedges,
    grapefruit wedges, cucumber twists, chilli slices, herb
    sprigs, juniper berries, coriander seeds, black peppercorns,
    cinnamon sticks, vanilla pods, lavender sprigs…

Instructions
Fill a highball or copa glass with ice and add your garnish, then pour in the gin and top up with tonic water.

NEGRONI

I was introduced to the Negroni by my friend Sara Ross
on a trip to her family's home city of Genoa. It was my
first trip to Italy, and before taking us out to eat our body
weight in pasta, Sara told us it was important to warm
up with a Negroni. Ice cold, sharp and shocking, it's one
of the few drinks that really will perk up your taste buds
and get your stomach revved up, ready for dinner.
Making a good Negroni depends on the ingredients.
Campari is inevitable. The gin should be a strong London
dry gin – minimum 40% ABV so it has enough heft to grapple
with the flavours of the Campari and the vermouth. For
the sweet vermouth, I like Punt e Mes, which has notes of
dark chocolate mixed in with its weed-like tangle of herbal
bitters. For something a little lighter, try Cinzano Rosso.

Ingredients
22ml (¾fl oz) sweet vermouth
22ml (¾fl oz) Campari
22ml (¾fl oz) London dry gin
an orange slice, to garnish

Instructions
Fill an old fashioned glass with ice and pour in the
vermouth, then the Campari and then the gin. Briefly
stir, then tuck in a slice of orange and serve.

NEGRONI

GIN RICKEY

Nowhere is summer hotter, stickier or muggier than in
the swamps of Washington DC when there is an election
campaign on. Back in 1883, after celebrating the election
of his favourite candidate for House Speaker, Democratic
lobbyist Colonel Joe Rickey walked into Shoomaker's bar
and invented the Rickey. He instructed the bartender
George Williamson to mix rye whiskey, lime juice and soda
together to make a refreshing summer drink that was as
good for hangovers as it was for thirst. The Colonel stayed
true to rye, but the crowd at Shoomaker's liked gin better.

Ingredients
juice of 1 lime
60ml (2fl oz) gin
120ml (4fl oz) soda water
a lime wedge, to garnish

Instructions
Half fill a highball glass with ice and pour in the lime juice. Top
up with gin and then soda water. Give it a brief stir, then drop in
a lime wedge to garnish.

RED SNAPPER

I've never really liked Bloody Marys. Too often they're
so laden with vodka, horseradish and Tabasco sauce
that they taste like drinking the aftermath of a nuclear
explosion. I consigned them to the drinks cabinet marked
'not for me'. Then I spent a day making cocktails at the
Hotel du Vin in Brighton, under the tutelage of head
barman Ben Manchester. He showed me the secret
to a good Bloody Mary was to use less tomato juice,
more Worcestershire sauce, just a hum of Tabasco
heat and – very crucially – swap the vodka for gin.

Ingredients
60ml (2fl oz) gin
120ml (4fl oz) tomato juice
15ml (½fl oz) freshly squeezed lemon juice
8ml (¼fl oz) Amontillado sherry
4 dashes of Worcestershire sauce
5 generous dashes of Tabasco sauce
2 pinches of celery salt
a pinch of freshly ground black pepper
a lime wedge and a celery stick, to garnish

Instructions
Half fill a shaker with ice. Pour in the gin, tomato juice,
lemon juice, sherry, Worcestershire sauce, Tabasco sauce,
celery salt and black pepper. Seal and very gently slide
the liquids back and forwards in the shaker for around
1 minute to chill them without shaking them (drinking frothy
tomato juice is not so pleasant). Half fill a large highball
glass with ice and double strain the Red Snapper into the
glass. Garnish with a lime wedge and a celery stick.

ROSE'S

LIME JUICE
CORDIAL
L. ROSE & Co
LONDON

SAILOR'S
FRIEND

DELICIOUS, WHOLESOME & REFRESHING

GIMLET

Sometimes cocktails are not just cocktails. Sometimes they save lives. In the 18th century, scurvy killed more British sailors than enemy cannons. The on-board diet of hardtack (biscuits) and salted meat left sailors vitamin-deficient and they died in their thousands until Scottish surgeon James Lind demonstrated that a daily dose of lime juice prevented scurvy taking hold. But how to get the lime juice into the sailors? Fresh limes didn't last long at sea, and the crews weren't keen on the sour flavour. Naturally, the British Navy turned to alcohol. First by mixing lime juice with rum, then by carrying bottles of Rose's Lime Cordial, a mix of lime juice and sugar that the sailors stirred into gin. The classic recipe is fifty-fifty navy strength gin and lime cordial, but I like adding a sharpening splash of fresh juice to the mix.

Ingredients
60ml (2fl oz) Plymouth navy strength gin
45ml (1 ½fl oz) Rose's Lime Cordial
22ml (¾fl oz) freshly squeezed lime juice
a maraschino cherry, to garnish

Instructions
Half fill a mixing glass with ice. Add all the ingredients and stir together for around 30 seconds. Strain into a coupe glass and drop in a maraschino cherry to garnish.

HANKY PANKY

Ada 'Coley' Coleman was the first female head bartender at The Savoy's American Bar. She started her career at Claridge's in 1899. Her father had worked for Rupert D'Oyly Carte, and when he died, D'Oyly Carte offered Coley a bar job. Her talent for mixing drinks got her noticed and in 1903 The Savoy tempted her to join their bar crew. In the American Bar she made cocktails for actors, musicians, writers and royalty. One actor who came her way was the silent movie star Charles Hawtrey. In an interview with *The Daily Express* in 1925, Coley explained how she'd come up with a new cocktail for him: 'The late Charles Hawtrey... was one of the best judges of cocktails that I knew. Some years ago, when he was over working, he used to come into the bar and say, "Coley, I am tired. Give me something with a bit of punch in it." It was for him that I spent hours experimenting until I had invented a new cocktail. The next time he came in, I told him I had a new drink for him. He sipped it, and, draining the glass, he said, "By Jove! That is the real hanky-panky!" And Hanky Panky it has been called ever since.'

Ingredients
45ml (1½fl oz) London dry gin
45ml (1½fl oz) sweet vermouth
2 dashes of Fernet-Branca (a bitter herbal liqueur)
an orange twist, to garnish

Instructions
Fill a mixing glass with ice. Add all the ingredients and stir together for around 30 seconds. Strain into a chilled martini glass and garnish with an orange twist.

SINGAPORE SLING

This was the first cocktail I ever drank, and I did drink it in Singapore. I was on a trip to New Zealand with the Girl Guides as a teenager. One of the highlights of our trip was visiting Raffles Hotel, where the Singapore Sling was invented by bartender Ngiam Tong Boon sometime between 1913 and 1915. No stopping for cocktails though: much too expensive for our teenage purses. Our chance would come at a much less reputable bar, on the last day of our trip. The Singapore Slings came garlanded with lemon slices, maraschino cherries, tiny umbrellas, twizzle sticks and straws. They were sweet and fruity and easy to drink, leaving me muzzy-headed and grinning. I was impressed and decided that cocktails and I were destined to get on. The recipe below is Raffles Hotel's official version of the drink.

Ingredients
30ml (1fl oz) London dry gin
15ml (½fl oz) Cherry Heering Liqueur
8ml (¼fl oz) Cointreau
8ml (¼fl oz) Bénédictine D.O.M. liqueur
120ml (4fl oz) freshly squeezed pineapple juice
15ml (½fl oz) freshly squeezed lime juice
10ml (¼fl oz) grenadine
1 dash of Angostura bitters
mint leaves, a lemon slice and a maraschino cherry, to garnish

Instructions
Pour all the ingredients into an ice-filled cocktail shaker and shake vigorously. Fill a tall glass with ice and strain in the cocktail. Garnish with a few sprigs of mint, a lemon slice and a maraschino cherry (and a cocktail umbrella if, like me, you can't resist them).

PINK GIN

The colour in this cocktail comes from the Angostura bitters, the best known of the herbal tonics, which give cocktails some of their sass. Angostura bitters were invented by Johann Gottlieb Benjamin Siegert, a German doctor who settled in a small Venezuelan town called Angostura and experimented with the local plant life to make tonics and medicines. In 1820, he created a herbal brew and marketed it to visiting sailors as a cure for seasickness. A British ship surgeon picked up a few bottles when he was in port and tried mixing them with gin. The pale pink aromatic drink was a hit, and by the middle of the 19th century, Pink Gins were being poured in bars on land as well as at sea.

Ingredients
3 dashes of Angostura bitters
50ml (1¾fl oz) Plymouth navy strength gin
a lemon twist, to garnish

Instructions
Half fill a mixing glass with ice. Add the Angostura bitters to the glass and stir for around 15 seconds. Strain off any excess water and bitters (a little will be left coating the ice and glass). Add the gin to the mixing glass and stir for 30 seconds. Strain into a chilled martini glass and garnish with a lemon twist.

BEES KNEES

This is a Prohibition-era cocktail straight from the speakeasies of 1920s America. It's a kind of gin sour, but with honey syrup adding a balancing dash of sweetness instead of the usual sugar syrup. The honey and the citrus juices would also have helped make the bootleg gin taste a little nicer back in the '20s.

Ingredients
2 tsp runny honey
2 tsp hot water
45ml (1½fl oz) London dry gin
15ml (½fl oz) freshly squeezed lemon juice
15ml (½fl oz) freshly squeezed orange juice
an orange twist, to garnish

Instructions
Stir the honey and hot water together in a shaker to dissolve the honey. Fill the shaker with ice. Pour in the gin, lemon and orange juice. Shake together vigorously, then strain into a martini glass. Garnish with an orange twist.

GIN ALEXANDER

When you think of an Alexander, you probably think of a Brandy Alexander. But the original recipe was made with gin mixed in equal quantities with crème de cacao and cream. It first appeared in Hugo R. Ensslin's 1917 *Recipes for Mixed Drinks*, although Ensslin left out the identity of the Alexander the drink was named after. It might have been Philadelphia baseball pitcher Grover Cleveland Alexander, who played in the team that beat Boston in the 1915 World Series. The head bartender at The Racquet Club was said to be so delighted with the team's success, he celebrated the best way he knew how – with a drink. Another claimant is Troy Alexander, a bartender at a ritzy New York lobster restaurant who wanted to impress a group of railway investors by serving them a perfect, pure white cocktail.

Ingredients
45ml (1½fl oz) Old Tom gin
30ml (1fl oz) crème de cacao
22ml (¾fl oz) single cream
15ml (½fl oz) egg white
nutmeg, for grating, to garnish

Instructions
Half fill a shaker with ice. Pour in the gin, crème de cacao and cream and shake well to chill. Strain into a mixing glass, throw the ice out of the shaker and then pour the cocktail mix back in. Add the egg white and shake again for 30 seconds. Strain into a coupe glass and grate over a little nutmeg to serve.

ALABAMA SLAMMER

In the 1980s, Alabama Slammers were so popular they even got a namecheck in *Cocktail*, the movie that brought us Tom Cruise in a skinny tie and white shirt, spinning shakers and twirling bottles to nightclubs full of adoring barflies. Sweet, fruity and about as subtle as Cruise's pouring technique, the Alabama Slammer seems to have originated at the University of Alabama in the 1970s, when it was drunk as a shot. Made into a long drink with orange juice, it's refreshing and surprisingly moreish. I like it with brunch on hot summer weekends.

Ingredients
30ml (1fl oz) Sloe Gin (see page 14)
30ml (1fl oz) Southern Comfort
30ml (1fl oz) amaretto
60ml (2fl oz) freshly squeezed orange juice
an orange slice and a maraschino cherry, to garnish

Instructions
Half fill a shaker with ice. Pour in all the ingredients and shake vigorously. Fill a tall glass with ice and strain in the cocktail. Garnish with a slice of orange and a maraschino cherry.

FIN DE SIÈCLE

The name Fin de Siècle seems to have been used for a
couple of different cocktails, all mixed towards the end
of the 19th century when the phrase was in vogue and
drinkers were feeling grand, nostalgic and a little bit
contemplative. This recipe belongs to the same class of
proto-martinis as the Martinez (see page 40) and the Gin
& It (see page 32). Dry, herbal and with a lingering dash
of bitter orange zest from the Amer Picon (a bittersweet
orange aperitif), it's good both as an aperitif or digestif. If
you can't find Amer Picon, you can sub in Amaro CioCiaro.

Ingredients
45ml (1 ½fl oz) London dry gin
15ml (½fl oz) sweet vermouth
8ml (¼fl oz) Amer Picon or Amaro CioCiaro
1 dash of orange bitters
an orange twist, to garnish

Instructions
Half fill a mixing glass with ice. Add all the ingredients
and stir together for 30 seconds. Strain into a chilled
martini glass and serve with an orange twist.

Fin de Siècle

SATAN'S WHISKERS

There are two ways Satan wears his whiskers: straight or curled. They're straight when this fruity, orange-scented cocktail is made with Grand Marnier. And if you swap the Grand Marnier for orange curaçao, then those whiskers are curled.

Ingredients
15ml (½fl oz) London dry gin
15ml (½fl oz) dry vermouth
15ml (½fl oz) sweet vermouth
15ml (½fl oz) freshly squeezed orange juice
8ml (¼fl oz) Grand Marnier or curaçao
3 dashes of orange bitters
an orange twist, to garnish

Instructions
Half fill a shaker with ice. Add all the ingredients and shake together really well. Strain into a martini glass and serve with an orange twist.

FRENCH 75

The Soixante-Quinze was a 75-millimetre light field gun
used by the French army in the First World War. It was a
powerful weapon, firing 15 rounds a minute, and is supposed
to be the inspiration behind this crisp, fizzy cocktail. One
legend has French troops sitting in their trenches with all the
ingredients to mix the cocktail – including the Champagne
– but no glasses, so they served them in empty 75mm shells.
Except the first published recipe for the 75 doesn't include
Champagne (or French soldiers living it up). Instead, it
shakes up brandy, gin, grenadine and lemon juice. A few
more evolutions occur until, in 1927, the familiar mix of gin,
Champagne, lemon juice and sugar came together. Unlike
the modern version of the drink, which is served in a flute, this
1920s French 75 is served in a tall glass over plenty of ice.

Ingredients
35ml (1¼fl oz) freshly squeezed lemon juice
3 tsp caster sugar
45ml (1½fl oz) London dry gin
90ml (3fl oz) brut Champagne
a lemon slice, to garnish

Instructions
Stir the lemon juice and sugar together in a cocktail shaker
until the sugar dissolves. Add ice and the gin and shake
together well. Fill a tall glass with ice and strain in the gin mix.
Top up with Champagne and garnish with a slice of lemon.

ZAZA

There were two things the Queen Mother considered essential when packing for her holidays: gin and Dubonnet. Mixed together, they make a cocktail called the Zaza. Or they did until the Queen Mum became so closely associated with the drink that some bar menus changed the drink's name to The Queen Mother. Typically, the Zaza is served straight up in a chilled martini glass, but the Queen Mum preferred to drink it stirred on the rocks and who am I to argue with such expertise? Easy to make, easy to drink and fiendishly strong, this cocktail is a lot of fun just as long as you treat it with plenty of respect. So, just like the real Queen Mum, then.

Ingredients
60ml (2fl oz) London dry gin
60ml (2fl oz) Dubonnet Red
a lemon twist, to garnish

Instructions
Fill a mixing glass with ice and add the gin and Dubonnet. Stir for around 30 seconds. Fill a small old fashioned glass with ice and strain the cocktail in. Garnish with a lemon twist.

GIN HOT TODDY

Good news! There is a cure for the common cold, and its name is gin. Not that you can apply gin to your cold in any old fashion and expect your symptoms to clear up. You have to do it in the right way. You have to do it in a hot toddy. Whenever I start to feel the cotton wool fogginess of a cold descending, I prescribe myself two Gin Hot Toddies before bed (never more nor less). In the morning I wake up free from coughs, sneezes, sniffles and soreness and I'm grateful to gin all over again.

Ingredients
35ml (1¼fl oz) Clementine Gin (see page 14)
juice of 1 clementine
1 tsp runny honey
1 cinnamon stick
4 cloves
1 orange slice
150ml (5fl oz) hot water

Instructions
Pour the gin and clementine juice into a heatproof glass or mug. Stir in the honey to dissolve it. Drop in the cinnamon stick. Stick the cloves into the orange slice and drop it into the mug. Top up with just boiled hot water, stirring a few times with the cinnamon stick to mix, and then serve.

SLOEGRONI

This wintry Negroni swaps London dry gin for sloe gin, which you would think would make it sweeter and easier to drink. In fact, the syrupy richness of the sloe gin helps the herbal flavours in the Campari and vermouth to bloom, giving the drink a lash of bitterness that sweeps across your tongue and shakes your taste buds alive. I love drinking it, ice cold and biting, curled up in front of a fire while the dark winter daylight fades away into the night.

Ingredients
22ml (¾fl oz) sweet vermouth
22ml (¾fl oz) Campari
22ml (¾fl oz) Sloe Gin (see page 14)
an orange slice, to garnish

Instructions
Fill an old fashioned glass with ice and pour in the sweet vermouth, then the Campari and then the Sloe Gin. Stir a few times to mix, tuck in a slice of orange and serve.

RAMBLE

If Dick Bradsell created the Bramble (see page 35) to commemorate the blackberry bushes of his Isle of Wight childhood, then I've created this riff on it to remember day trips to the pick-your-own farms of my youth. The trips to those farms all went the same way. We would arrive and be given boxes, which we would fill with strawberries, raspberries, black and red currants, as well as filling our own bellies as we picked. We can't have been the only family who arrived at the cash desk with mucky-mouthed kids beaming red-stained smiles. Everybody queuing to pay had berry-filled bellies poking out from under their T-shirts, with red juices staining their fingers the same way the crème de framboise stains the ice in this drink.

Ingredients
60ml (2fl oz) Raspberry Gin (see page 13)
45ml (1½fl oz) freshly squeezed lemon juice
30ml (1fl oz) Simple Syrup (see page 15)
30ml (1fl oz) crème de framboise
a couple of raspberries, to garnish

Instructions
Fill an old fashioned glass with crushed ice. Pour the gin, lemon juice and Simple Syrup over the ice and gently stir together. Top up the crushed ice so it fills the glass again. Pour the crème de framboise over the top so it 'bleeds' down into the drink. Garnish with a couple of raspberries and serve with two short straws (the straws are optional – they help to mix the drink so the first sip isn't just a mouthful of framboise, but plastic straws are so bad for the environment you might prefer to skip the straw and give the drink a bit of a stir to mix it all together before drinking).

SLOE GIN FIZZ

A classic mid-19th-century cocktail, the Gin Fizz comes in many guises. There are Silver Fizzes with added egg white, Royal Fizzes with whole eggs mixed in, the famous Ramos Gin Fizz, which features cream, orange flower water and lime juice amongst its ingredients, and then there is this pale purple Sloe Gin Fizz, which swaps dry gin for sweet, hedgerow-scented sloe gin. A tall sour, it's a great summer cocktail.

Ingredients
60ml (2fl oz) Sloe Gin (see page 14)
30ml (1fl oz) freshly squeezed lemon juice
8ml (¼fl oz) Simple Syrup (see page 15)
soda water, to top up
a lemon wedge and a mint sprig, to garnish

Instructions
Pour the Sloe Gin, lemon juice and Simple Syrup into an ice-filled cocktail shaker. Shake together well. Fill a tall glass with ice, strain in the gin mix, then top up with soda water for the fizz. Garnish with a wedge of lemon and a sprig of fresh mint.

HURLY BURLY

My friend Emily Georghiou invented this drink on a long weekend at the Latitude Music Festival in Suffolk. She travelled there in a camper van, which came with a lot of benefits – a real bed to sleep in, a little kitchen to cook in and a small icebox where Emily kept bottles of ginger ale cool. Somehow, over the course of that long, hot July weekend, Emily ended up mixing gin with Chambord and ginger ale to take the heat out of the day. Dry, crisp and thirst-quenching, this cocktail quickly became her drink of the summer. Needing a name for it, she christened it the Hurly Burly after the festival's circus tent.

Ingredients
35ml (1¼fl oz) London dry gin
35ml (1¼fl oz) Chambord black raspberry liqueur
120ml (4fl oz) ginger ale

Instructions
Fill a highball glass with ice. Pour in the gin and Chambord. Give it a brief stir. Top up with the ginger ale and serve.

RHUBARB G&T

In an especially atmospheric corner of Soho in London, sits Bob Bob Ricard; or perhaps I should say reclines – Bob Bob Ricard is far too glamorous a restaurant to do anything as pedestrian as sit. Glitzy, gaudy, shimmering with mirrors and gilt, Bob Bob Ricard injects a little fabulousness into everything it does, including their signature cocktail: the Rhubarb G&T. The mix of sweetly moreish rhubarb gin with astringent tonic is beautifully refreshing, and easy to replicate at home. Make sure you use a good tonic water. Being more like Bob Bob Ricard means only using the best.

Ingredients
60ml (2fl oz) Rhubarb Gin (see page 13)
60ml (2fl oz) tonic water
4 dashes of rhubarb bitters
an orange wedge, to garnish

Instructions
Fill an old fashioned glass with ice, then pour in the Rhubarb Gin and top up with tonic water. Shake in 4 dashes of bitters and give it a brief stir. Lightly squeeze an orange wedge over the top, then tuck the wedge into the glass and serve.

LA COMTESSE

In Italy a Negroni Sbagliato is a 'mistaken' Negroni with the gin replaced by Prosecco, which does seem like a mistake. So I thought: if you're going to make a mistake, why not go all out? I swapped all the Italian ingredients for a mixture of dry French aperitif wine, chocolate and spice-scented French red vermouth, an acidic swirl of Champagne, and I kept in the gin. Every element a mistake, but such a good mistake.

Ingredients
22ml (¾fl oz) Old Tom gin
22ml (¾fl oz) Lillet Blanc
22ml (¾fl oz) Noilly Prat Rouge (French sweet vermouth)
120ml (4fl oz) brut Champagne
an orange twist, to garnish

Instructions
Fill a shaker with ice and pour in the gin, Lillet Blanc and Noilly Prat Rouge. Shake vigorously for 30 seconds, then strain into a coupe glass. Top up with Champagne. Garnish with an orange twist to serve.

SLOE GIN HOT CHOCOLATE

(Serves 2)

Pure indulgence. There's no other way to describe this drink. Thick, rich and creamy, with a lingering, chest-warming burn of booze from the sloe gin. It's the kind of drink that makes you hope for bleak winter days, packed with snow and ice, so you can justify making it.

Ingredients

50g (1¾oz) dark chocolate
50g (1¾oz) milk chocolate
500ml (17fl oz) whole milk
½ tsp ground cinnamon
a pinch of sea salt
70ml (2¼fl oz) Sloe Gin (see page 14)
cocoa powder, for dusting

Instructions

Finely chop the dark and milk chocolate, and set aside. Pour the milk into a saucepan and place over a low heat. Gently stir now and then, until the pan is steaming hot, but not boiling. Add the chopped chocolate, ground cinnamon and salt. Stir until the chocolate has melted and the hot chocolate is smooth and rich. Taste and add a little more cinnamon or salt to taste. Divide the Sloe Gin between 2 mugs, then top up with the hot chocolate. Dust with a little cocoa powder and serve.

SLOE GIN SOUR

I'm going to describe this as a very Christmassy drink. Not
that you should limit yourself to drinking it at Christmas.
In fact, the bright citrusy flavours would be delightful
on any sunny afternoon. But it's the combination of
sloes and clementines in it that makes me think of dark
December days, twinkling lights, tinsel and mistletoe. And
also how it looks in the glass: a royal purple drink with
a layer of snowy white foam on top. There's something
very celebratory about it that somehow, I reckon, it could
turn any event into the most wonderful day of the year.

Ingredients
45ml (1½fl oz) Sloe Gin (see page 14)
15ml (½fl oz) Clementine Gin (see page 14)
15ml (½fl oz) freshly squeezed lemon juice
15ml (½fl oz) egg white
an orange twist, to garnish

Instructions
Pour the Sloe Gin, Clementine Gin and lemon juice into
a cocktail shaker. Add ice and shake vigorously for 30
seconds, then strain into a glass. Discard the ice and
pour the cocktail back into the shaker along with the
egg white. Shake again for 30 seconds. Strain into a
chilled coupe glass and garnish with an orange twist.

SOUTH
TYROL

BIRTHPLACE OF BLUSHING HUGO

BLUSHING HUGO

There are benefits to having friends living in different cities around the world. Not least, free holiday accommodation and the opportunity to seek out new drinks. Visiting my friend Gill Hall in Switzerland a few years ago, I expected to enjoy clean mountain air, piles of cheese and an efficient public transportation system. I hadn't expected to find a cocktail I'd never tried before: the Hugo. This variation on a spritz was invented in South Tyrol in the Italian Alps by Roland Gruber, a barman who wanted to offer his patrons something different to the ever popular Aperol Spritz. His original recipe used Prosecco, tonic water, lemon balm syrup and freshly squeezed lemon juice. The drink, first mixed in 2011, quickly took off and travelled around Germany and Switzerland, somehow swapping elderflower syrup for the lemon balm along the way. When I drank my first Hugo with Gill at a pavement café by the Limmat river in Zurich, we agreed that it was delicious, but that what it could really do with was a little extra gin.

Ingredients
120ml (4fl oz) brut Prosecco
30ml (1fl oz) Rhubarb Gin (see page 13)
15ml (½fl oz) elderflower cordial
60ml (2fl oz) soda water
fresh mint sprigs and a lime wedge, to garnish

Instructions
Half fill a large wine glass with ice. Pour in the Prosecco, then pour the Rhubarb Gin and elderflower cordial over the top. Give it a brief stir. Top up with the soda water and tuck a few mint sprigs and a lime wedge into the glass to serve.

ENGLISH 75

I can't think of three more English drinks than tea, gin and sparkling wine (in spite of none of them having their origins in England). The whole world knows how much we love a cup of tea, and also a glass of gin. Sparkling wine might seem more French than English, but the English are the reason there is fizz in your Champagne. In the 17th century, Champagne wine producers shipped barrels of white wine to England as soon as the initial fermentation had ceased. But in London's warm taverns a second fermentation would take place, creating the fizz. The French wine producers despaired, calling it the Devil's Wine, but the English drinkers loved it. And now we even have our own vineyards producing English fizz with the same biscuity snap as French Champagne. Combined with the tannic flavour of Earl Grey gin, and a floral dash of elderflower, it makes a deliciously English drink.

Ingredients
45ml (1½fl oz) Earl Grey Gin (see page 14)
8ml (¼fl oz) elderflower cordial
15ml (½fl oz) freshly squeezed lemon juice
75ml (2½fl oz) English sparkling wine

Instructions
Fill a shaker with ice and pour in the gin, elderflower cordial and lemon juice. Shake together vigorously, then strain into a flute. Carefully pour in half the chilled sparkling wine and give it a little stir, then top up with the rest of the sparkling wine and serve.

GENEVER FLIP

The first flips appeared in taverns in the 1690s, when barkeepers stirred together ale, rum, molasses and egg and then plunged a red-hot poker into the drink to make it froth (or flip). This hearty mix helped drinkers keep out the cold until the late 19th century, when American bartenders got hold of the drink and started creating chilled versions. There's a debate as to whether a flip should include cream or not, but I've added it here as it rounds out the drink and adds a layer of extra richness that I can't resist.

Ingredients
60ml (2fl oz) oude genever
15ml (½fl oz) Simple Syrup (see page 15)
15ml (½fl oz) single cream
1 egg
nutmeg, for grating, to garnish

Instructions
Pour the genever, Simple Syrup and cream into a cocktail shaker. Crack in the egg. Shake vigorously for 30 seconds, then add ice and shake again. Strain into a coupe glass and grate over a little nutmeg to serve.

YUZU SOUR

The size of a tangerine, covered in knobbly skin and full of pips, the yuzu doesn't look terribly promising, but its tart, floral juice tastes like an aromatic cross between lemons and limes, which makes it perfect for mixing in cocktails, like this classic gin sour.

Ingredients
60ml (2fl oz) London dry gin
30ml (1fl oz) yuzu juice
8ml (¼fl oz) Simple Syrup (see page 15)
3 dashes of yuzu bitters
15ml (½fl oz) egg white
a lime or yuzu twist, to garnish

Instructions
Pour the gin, yuzu juice and Simple Syrup into a cocktail shaker. Add the yuzu bitters and the egg white and shake vigorously for 30 seconds. Add ice and shake again for 30 seconds. Strain into a chilled coupe glass and garnish with a lime or yuzu twist.

ORIGINAL

RECIPE

ADVOCAAT

PRODUCT
OF
HOLLAND

17.2% vol   70cl

FLUFFY DUCKLING

The Fluffy Duck is one of those 1980s cocktails that makes you wonder just how drunk everyone was in the '80s. Who was sat in a bar and thought: 'I know! Gin, Advocaat and orange juice! That'll be a great drink.' Crazy as they were, they were also right. The hint of almond in the Advocaat marries up neatly with the citrus in the triple sec and the orange juice's fresh zing, creating a light, appealing cocktail with a smooth finish. I've swapped in clementine gin and juice and, as clementines are that bit smaller than oranges, I decided it has to be called a Fluffy Duckling.

Ingredients
45ml (1½fl oz) Clementine Gin (see page 14)
45ml (1½fl oz) Advocaat
45ml (1½fl oz) triple sec
45ml (1½fl oz) freshly squeezed clementine juice
soda water, to top up
an orange slice, to garnish

Instructions
Fill a shaker with ice and pour in the Clementine Gin, Advocaat, triple sec and clementine juice. Shake vigorously to mix. Fill a highball glass with ice and strain in the cocktail. Top up with a little soda water and garnish with an orange slice.

YANGON BLUEBIRD

I love a blue cocktail, and I don't think I'm alone in that. I've seen more and more blue cocktails appearing on bar menus in London, and that makes me glad. After years of being very serious about cocktails, bartenders are finally letting a little silliness creep back into the mix. This particular blue cocktail is based on the signature drink of the Pegu Club – a colonial drinking establishment set up for British expats in Rangoon (now Yangon), Burma. In spite of its ridiculous colour, this cocktail is actually a very serious-tasting drink, with a tongue-scraping hit of citrus and a clean martini finish.

Ingredients
60ml (2fl oz) London dry gin
22ml (¾fl oz) blue curaçao
22ml (¾fl oz) freshly squeezed lime juice
8ml (¼fl oz) Simple Syrup (see page 15)
1 dash of Angostura bitters
1 dash of orange bitters
a grapefruit twist, to garnish

Instructions
Fill a shaker with ice and pour in the gin, blue curaçao, lime juice and Simple Syrup. Add a dash each of Angostura and orange bitters and shake together. Strain into a martini glass and garnish with a grapefruit twist.

Aged Genever
Amsterdam
est. 1575

BARREL AGED FOR
18 MONTHS

GENEVER OLD FASHIONED

Did you pick up this book by accident and are now remembering that you don't actually like gin? Don't worry. This cocktail is for you. The drink's full name is The Old Fashioned Whiskey Cocktail and it dates from the very start of the cocktail-making era. In the early 1800s it was served in the morning as an eye-opener. These days, thanks to the TV show *Mad Men*, it's popular with drinkers looking for something elegant with a little old-world cool. Oude genever, with its rich, malty flavour, is the perfect stand-in for whiskey, especially if you pick a barrel-aged variety.

Ingredients
1 tsp Demerara sugar
1 tsp water
2 dashes of Angostura bitters
60ml (2fl oz) barrel-aged oude genever
a maraschino cherry and an orange twist, to garnish

Instructions
Add the sugar, water and bitters to an old fashioned glass and stir together to dissolve the sugar. Add the genever with ice and stir for around 30 seconds. Garnish with a maraschino cherry and an orange twist.

GENEVER SAZERAC

The Sazerac is the official cocktail of New Orleans. Originally made with Cognac, bartenders moved onto making them with rye whiskey when Cognac supplies grew scarce in the 1870s. From rye, it's not such a jump to oude genever. Barley-based, full of honey notes and autumn spice, oude genever has just the right flavour profile for this simple mixed drink. And even though it has its origins in steamy, subtropical New Orleans, this is a drink that tastes like winter firesides to me.

Ingredients
60ml (2fl oz) oude genever
8ml (¼fl oz) Simple Syrup (see page 15)
1 dash of Angostura bitters
3 dashes of Peychaud's bitters
1 tsp absinthe
a lemon twist, to garnish

Instructions
Fill an old fashioned glass with ice and set aside for 15 minutes to chill. Once it has chilled, fill a separate old fashioned glass with ice and add the genever, Simple Syrup and both bitters. Stir for about 15 seconds. This is your Sazerac mix. Set aside. Take the ice-filled glass and tip out the ice. Add the absinthe to the chilled glass and roll it around the glass to coat the inside. Shake out any excess. Add more ice, then strain your Sazerac mix into the glass. Garnish with a lemon twist.

LOVE IN THE MIST

The name of this cocktail is, I admit, a bit cutesy. But when you make it, and see the pale pink tendrils of rhubarb gin uncurling in the misty white mix of Cointreau and lemon juice, you'll have to admit that I couldn't call it anything else.

Ingredients
45ml (1½fl oz) Rhubarb Gin (see page 13)
22ml (¾fl oz) Cointreau
15ml (½fl oz) freshly squeezed lemon juice
1 dash of rhubarb bitters
1 drop of orange blossom water
an orange twist, to garnish

Instructions
Fill a shaker with ice. Pour in all the ingredients (making sure to just use a drop of the orange blossom water) and shake well together. Strain into a small coupe glass and garnish with an orange twist.

SALTY SEA DOG

The Salty Dog is a cocktail from the 1960s that simply combined vodka with grapefruit juice and maraschino liqueur and served it in a salt-rimmed glass. Refreshing, easy to make and with a lip-tingling mix of salt and sour to keep it interesting. But, since everything is better made with gin, I've swapped the vodka for Plymouth navy strength gin. As the gin is stronger, I've changed it from a long drink served over ice, to a straight up cocktail that you can sip while waiting for your ship to come in.

Ingredients
1 lime wedge
crushed sea salt, to dip the rim
60ml (2fl oz) Plymouth navy strength gin
1 tsp maraschino liqueur
2 dashes of orange bitters
45ml (1 ½fl oz) pink grapefruit juice
a grapefruit twist, to garnish

Instructions
Rub the rim of a coupe glass with the lime wedge, then dip it in crushed sea salt to lightly coat. Set aside. Fill a shaker with ice and add the gin, maraschino liqueur, bitters and grapefruit juice. Squeeze the lime wedge into the shaker, then shake all the ingredients together. Strain into the salt-rimmed glass and garnish with a grapefruit twist.

the salty
sea dog

SCARLET & BLACK

I use black pepper every day when I'm cooking, but I almost never think about it by itself. I consider it as an enhancer, but black peppercorns have an appeal of their own. A warm, cutting heat that has started to make its way into gin as part of the bushels of botanicals used during the distilling process. Black pepper's hot astringency makes it a natural complement to juicy raspberries. The peppercorns' sharpness brings out their sweetness and adds layers of flavour to this sparkling cocktail.

Ingredients
2 black peppercorns
45ml (1 ½fl oz) Raspberry Gin (see page 13)
15ml (½fl oz) freshly squeezed lime juice
a drop of rosewater
Champagne, to top up
a couple of raspberries, to garnish

Instructions
Put the peppercorns in a cocktail shaker and use a muddler to crush them. (Alternatively, grind the peppercorns in a pestle and mortar and drop into a cocktail shaker.) Add ice, gin, lime and rosewater (make sure it is just a drop; a little goes a long way with rosewater). Shake together vigorously, then strain into a flute. Top up with the Champagne (add a little to start, give it a gentle stir, then top up the glass). Drop in the raspberries to garnish, and serve.

BLOOD ON THE DANCE FLOOR

In 1922 a movie was released that starred Rudolph Valentino as a poor boy who grew up to be the greatest matador in all of Spain. It was called *Blood and Sand* and a London bartender was so impressed with the film, he created a cocktail to honour it. Equal parts whiskey, Cherry Heering liqueur, sweet vermouth and orange juice, it's a cocktail steeped in metaphor (the Cherry Heering liqueur is meant to be the blood while the orange juice is the sand) and strong smoky flavours. My riff on it uses barrel-aged oude genever to give the drink a dash of oaky vanilla, and grapefruit juice for mouth-puckering sourness. Warning, the blood on the dance floor occurs after you've had a few of these and decide that you really are the best dancer in the world and everyone in the nightclub needs to see it.

Ingredients
30ml (1fl oz) barrel-aged oude genever
22ml (¾fl oz) Cherry Heering liqueur
22ml (¾fl oz) sweet vermouth
22ml (¾fl oz) freshly squeezed grapefruit juice
a maraschino cherry and an orange
   or grapefruit twist, to garnish

Instructions
Fill a cocktail shaker with ice. Pour in all the ingredients and shake well. Strain into a coupe glass and garnish with a maraschino cherry and an orange or grapefruit twist.

LONDON FOG CUTTER

It's hard to imagine anything further away from the grey and drizzly streets of London than a Tiki bar, and yet this cocktail, named after the thick layers of fog that once shrouded the UK's capital, is a Tiki drink. Tiki bars took California (and then the world) by storm in the 1930s. Bright, escapist pseudo Caribbean- and South Pacific-themed drinks like the Fog Cutter did wonders to sweep depression-era troubles away. This version swaps in a few English spirits to give the original tropical punch a lick of London attitude.

Ingredients

30ml (1fl oz) white rum
15ml (½fl oz) Earl Grey Gin (see page 14)
22ml (¾fl oz) cider brandy
15ml (½fl oz) freshly squeezed lemon juice
45ml (1½fl oz) freshly squeezed orange juice
15ml (½fl oz) orgeat (almond) syrup
15ml (½fl oz) Amontillado sherry
an orange twist and straws, to garnish

Instructions

Fill a shaker with ice and pour in the rum, Earl Grey Gin, cider brandy, lemon juice, orange juice and orgeat syrup. Shake well and strain into an ice-filled highball glass. Float the sherry on top by holding a teaspoon upside down over the top of the glass, then slowly pouring the sherry over it so it sits on top of the cocktail. Garnish with an orange twist and drink through a straw to avoid getting a mouthful of sherry and nothing else.

RASPBERRY AID

Sometimes all you want is a cheerful drink. Something colourful and bright – maybe hot pink – that is sweet and sharp, with a dash of lemon sherbet. Long enough to drink in gulps in the sunshine and strong enough to make you pause, slow down and savour the moment. This is that drink.

Ingredients
30ml (1fl oz) Raspberry Gin (see page 13)
30ml (1fl oz) limoncello
15ml (½fl oz) freshly squeezed lemon juice
15ml (½fl oz) Simple Syrup (see page 15)
120ml (4fl oz) soda water
a lemon slice, maraschino cherry and
    cocktail umbrella, to garnish

Instructions
Fill a highball glass with ice. Pour in the Raspberry Gin, limoncello, lemon juice and Simple Syrup. Stir a few times to mix well, then top up with soda water. Give it another stir. Garnish with a lemon slice and maraschino cherry on a cocktail stick and top with a cocktail umbrella.

MARGUERITTE

Daisies are not just cheerful flowers that brighten up lawns, they're also a type of cocktail that was popular in the 19th century. The first time they're mentioned in print is in the fabulously titled novel *Gay Life in New York, or Fast Men and Grass Widows*, which was published in 1866.

To be a Daisy, a drink must include a spirit, citrus juice, a sweetener and something to give it a little fizz. Gin seems like the obvious base spirit (of course) and I've added in some smooth French orange liqueur and blended it with almond-flavoured orgeat syrup. It's a fresh, invigorating cocktail that would be a natural fit at a summer picnic.

Ingredients
45ml (1½fl oz) Old Tom gin
15ml (½fl oz) Mandarine Napoleon liqueur
22ml (¾fl oz) freshly squeezed lemon juice
8ml (¼fl oz) orgeat (almond) syrup
a few dashes of soda water
a maraschino cherry and an orange twist, to garnish

Instructions
Fill a shaker with ice. Pour in the gin, Mandarine Napoleon liqueur, lemon juice and orgeat syrup. Shake vigorously and pour into a chilled coupe glass. Top with a few dashes of soda water, then drop in a maraschino cherry and an orange twist to serve.

CORIANDER & GINGER GIMLET

When I told people I was writing a book of gin cocktails, responses ranged from: 'Can I help you try out the recipes?' to 'Make me a cocktail with this in it!' My friend Gill Penlington asked for coriander, which was one of the nicer challenges I was set. So this grassy green gimlet is for Gill. It has a herbaceous flavour thanks to the fresh coriander, and a dry hint of lemon from the coriander seeds. Ginger and lime always get on well with coriander, so it seemed sensible to include them in the mix, with a dash of sugar syrup to even out the tartness.

Ingredients
4 fresh coriander sprigs
½ tsp coriander seeds
1 slice of fresh ginger
60ml (2fl oz) London dry gin
45ml (1½fl oz) freshly squeezed lime juice
8ml (¼fl oz) Simple Syrup (see page 15)
a maraschino cherry, to garnish

Instructions
Put the fresh coriander, coriander seeds and ginger in a cocktail shaker and use a muddler, pestle or the end of a wooden spoon to bash them together until the coriander is bruised and wilted. Pour in the gin, lime juice and Simple Syrup. Add ice and shake together well, then double strain into a chilled martini glass. Drop in a cherry and serve.

EARLY TO BED

(Serves 2)

Great for de-stressing after a long day at work, this cocktail combines the soothing apple-and-hay flavours of chamomile tea with the talcum powder softness of elderflower and Lillet Blanc. The teapot, cups and saucers are a bit gimmicky, but what's life if you can't pretend to be the Mad Hatter now and then?

Ingredients

1 chamomile tea bag
120ml (4fl oz) boiling water
1 tsp runny honey
90ml (3fl oz) gin
30ml (1fl oz) Lillet Blanc
15ml (½fl oz) elderflower cordial
8ml (¼fl oz) freshly squeezed lemon juice
2 lemon slices, to garnish

Instructions

Cover the chamomile tea bag with the boiling water in a teapot and let it steep for 10 minutes. Take out the tea bag, give it a squeeze and discard. Stir in the honey to dissolve it. Add plenty of ice, then pour in the gin, Lillet Blanc, elderflower cordial and lemon juice. Stir for about 15 seconds, then put the lid on the teapot. Fill 2 teacups with ice and tuck a lemon slice in each. Pour the cocktail into the teacups to serve.

LYCHEE MARTINI

The first lychee martini was mixed in Clay, a Korean restaurant in New York in 2001, and it's been a modern classic ever since. It's not, strictly speaking, a martini but gets its name from the Y-shaped martini glass it's served in. I've swapped the vermouth for a mix of crème de violette and lime juice to give the drink a powdery lilac colour and some sharpness to square up to the sweetness of the lychee syrup and liqueur.

Ingredients
60ml (2fl oz) London dry gin
30ml (1fl oz) syrup from a tin of lychees
15ml (½fl oz) lychee liqueur
8ml (¼fl oz) crème de violette
8ml (¼fl oz) freshly squeezed lime juice
a lychee, to garnish

Instructions
Fill a mixing glass with ice and pour in the gin, syrup, lychee liqueur, crème de violette and lime juice. Stir for 30 seconds, then strain the cocktail into a chilled martini glass and garnish with a lychee from the tin.

LYCHEE
LIQUEUR

20% abv
70cl

SHOOTING STAR MARTINI

The Pornstar Martini was created in 2002 by Douglas Ankrah at The Townhouse Bar in London and it is insanely popular, which I put down to it being fun. Seriously, who can resist a huge pink drink with a passion fruit half bobbing about in it like a fruity life raft and a shot of Prosecco on the side? I wanted to create a gin version and the rounded flavour of an Old Tom gin is a great fit. And since gin is better than vodka, I had to serve a shot of something better than Prosecco to go with it – Champagne it is then.

Ingredients
2 passion fruit
60ml (2fl oz) Old Tom gin
15ml (½fl oz) passion fruit liqueur
15ml (½fl oz) Simple Syrup (see page 15)
1 dash of vanilla extract
15ml (½fl oz) freshly squeezed orange juice
35ml (1¼fl oz) brut Champagne

Instructions
Halve the passion fruit and scoop the seeds and pulp from three of the halves into a cocktail shaker. Add the gin, passion fruit liqueur, Simple Syrup, vanilla extract, orange juice and ice. Shake together really, really well for 30 seconds to 1 minute, then strain the cocktail into a chilled coupe glass through a hawthorn strainer (the passion fruit will clog up the top of your cocktail shaker). Float the remaining passion fruit half in the drink as a garnish. Serve a shot of Champagne on the side and alternate sips of the martini with the Champagne.

MULLED SLOE GIN

(Serves 12)

Christmas without something mulled isn't Christmas.
The secret to getting this right is to heat it very gently
over an hour or two, which lets the flavours mingle
without cooking off too much of the alcohol.

Ingredients

600ml (20fl oz) Sloe Gin (see page 14)
3 litres (100fl oz) apple juice
2 lemons
12 cloves
2 cinnamon sticks
8 cardamom pods
4 clementines
25g (1oz) fresh ginger
freshly squeezed lemon juice, to taste

Instructions

Pour the Sloe Gin and apple juice into a saucepan. Slice the
lemons and stud a few of the slices with the cloves. Add to
the pan with the cinnamon sticks and cardamom pods. Slice
the clementines and ginger (you don't need to peel either)
and add to the pan. Put on a close-fitting lid and set the pan
over a low heat. Very gently warm for around 1½ hours – the
mulled gin should just be steaming hot when you take the lid
off. Taste and add lemon juice to balance out the sweetness
of the Sloe Gin, then ladle into heatproof glasses to serve.

MUMBAI MULE

(Serves 12)

This riff on a Moscow Mule is a brilliant party punch. The garnish is really important for this drink, so don't skip it. The scent of the lime, mint and red chilli that you breathe in as you take your first sip fills out the spicy flavours of the drink.

Ingredients
8 green cardamom pods
1 cinnamon stick
1 tbsp coriander seeds
120ml (4fl oz) water
125g (4oz) caster sugar
25g (1oz) fresh ginger, sliced
600ml (20fl oz) London dry gin
300ml (10fl oz) freshly squeezed lime juice (about 12 limes)
ginger beer, to top up
mint sprigs, sliced fresh red chilli and lime wedges, to garnish

Instructions
Start by making a spiced syrup: lightly crush the cardamom pods to open them up, and tip them into a dry pan with the cinnamon stick and coriander seeds. Toast for 2–3 minutes until fragrant. Add the water, sugar and ginger. Bring to the boil, then turn down the heat and simmer for 2 minutes. Take off the heat and leave to cool, then strain the syrup into a sterilised jar, seal and store in the fridge for up to 2 weeks.

Pour all the spiced syrup, the gin and lime juice into an ice-filled jug. Stir to combine and chill. Fill 12 tall glasses with ice and divide the mix between them. Top up with ginger beer and garnish with mint sprigs, lime wedges and slices of chilli.

SUMMER CUP

(Serves 12)

Great for an afternoon garden party when the sun is shining, and even when it's not. The Summer Cup mix will keep if you store it in a sterilised bottle, so if you don't need all of it for your party – or you're planning a party for one – you can just use what you need and keep the rest for later.

Ingredients
700ml (24fl oz) London dry gin
700ml (24fl oz) sweet vermouth
375ml (12½fl oz) triple sec
2 tbsp good balsamic vinegar
6 dashes of Angostura bitters
ginger beer, to top up
cucumber slices, lemon slices, mint or lemon
    verbena sprigs and raspberries, to garnish

Instructions
In a large jug, mix together the gin, sweet vermouth, triple sec, balsamic vinegar and Angostura bitters. Have a taste and add a little more of any of the ingredients to taste. Decant into a sterilised bottle and chill. When you're ready to serve, fill highball glasses with ice and tuck in slices of cucumber and lemon, a few sprigs of mint or lemon verbena and drop in a couple of raspberries. Pour the Summer Cup mix into the glasses and top up with ginger beer.

GARDENER'S PUNCH

(Serves 12)

Peaches and basil are an irresistible combination. They taste like summer in Italy and make a lusciously fragrant punch.

Ingredients
125g (4oz) caster sugar
120ml (4fl oz) water
10g (¼oz) fresh basil
750ml (26fl oz) chilled London dry gin
250ml (8½fl oz) chilled peach schnapps
750ml (26fl oz) chilled peach nectar
250ml (8½fl oz) freshly squeezed lime juice
1 litre (34fl oz) chilled soda water
lime slices, peach slices, raspberries,
    basil and mint leaves, to garnish

Instructions
Start by making a basil syrup: combine the sugar and water in a small saucepan. Gently heat, stirring until the sugar dissolves. Bring to the boil, then turn down the heat and simmer for 2 minutes. Take off the heat, drop in the basil and leave to cool and infuse. When the syrup is cold, strain it into a sterilised jar, discarding the basil, seal and store in the fridge for up to 2 weeks.

Pour all the basil syrup into a large jug or punch bowl. Add the gin, peach schnapps, peach nectar and lime juice and stir to mix well. Top up with soda water. Add slices of lime and peach, a few handfuls of raspberries and a couple of handfuls of basil and mint leaves. Give it a gentle stir, then pour or ladle into punch glasses and have ice on hand for people who want their punch a little chillier.

CLEMENTINE SPARKLER

(Serves 12)

My family love Christmas Day and we plan every meal and drink months in advance. This is my contribution to the brunch part of the day, when we have breakfast surrounded by wrapping paper (and maybe some boxes of chocolates we've already eaten). It's a kind of cross between a Mimosa and a French 75 with elements of Negroni Sbagliato thrown in for good measure. You can never have too much of a good thing at Christmas.

Ingredients
120ml (4fl oz) Clementine Gin (see page 14)
120ml (4fl oz) Campari
250ml (8½fl oz) freshly squeezed clementine juice
1 litre (34fl oz) Prosecco

Instructions
Pour 10ml (¼fl oz) Clementine Gin into 12 flutes. Layer 10ml (¼fl oz) Campari on top of each. Add 20ml (¾fl oz) clementine juice to each glass, then top up with chilled Prosecco, tilting the glasses a little so you can pour the fizz in without it foaming up over the top of the glass.

INDEX

142

CREDITS

Jassy Davis would like to thank:
Hazel Eriksson, who must be the most laidback editor in the world, and who made putting this book together extra easy. I had much too much fun writing this, and that's thanks to you.

Jennie and Jamie Brotherston, Nicola Swift, Francesca Burnett-Hall, Jordi Morrison, Emily Georghiou, Sara Ross, Joanne Bell and Gill Penlington, who all offered advice, provided inspiration and bravely volunteered to be guinea pigs when I needed people to try out the drinks. I salute you all. Warren Nettleford, who didn't mind bits of cocktail-making kit and strange spirits cluttering up the kitchen. Be glad you weren't home the day I made 20 cocktails in a row.

Gerry, Doug, Alex and Cara Davis – the original gin-drinking crew, my favourite critics and my best cheerleaders. This book is for you.

Ruby Taylor would like to thank:
Mum, Dad, Lucy, Izzy, Eddie and Aunty Hilary.